MW01273494

5 Minutes Day For Kids

Teach children to practice Gratitude and Mindfulness for everyday Happiness and Positiveness, Develop Positive Thinking

SHEILA ROSENBERG

Copyright © 2020 Sheila Rosenberg

All rights reserved.

ISBN: 9798616749048

CONTENTS

INTRODUCTION

The quote "Children is the future of a country" which have been counseling by our ancestor in the past is still truly a truth and never be considered old-fashioned. It is going to be easy to ruin a kid's feelings. In contrast, helping him or her in absorbing deeply moral principles that are imparted by adults and putting them into practical situations is a problematic issue that gets a lot of parent nerves to find out some solution. It may sound nonsense but there is a "inner power" to do something inside of children that we, especially parent can't break down, such as an ability to master a language of a kid since he or she was still a newborn child, their innocently easy-going attitude to pour and share their personal feeling, queries, even criticism and being sensitive so that his or her mind could be easily sculpted by those actions, sayings of parent, friends, and society. As a result, he or she would actualize his (her) thinking as well as gestures in the long run. Thereby, educating morality, behaviors, and the attitude of human beings since they were a child is always an urgent mission which is necessary for the government, society in general and particularly moms and dads to put on the top. This book seems to be a "relative firm suitcase" for those who are musing on looking for a way that could professionally "train" your kids, your nephews, your cousins and form a positive mindset in their head whereby they would make them become positive acts. The information in this book is limited by the lack of materials as well as knowledge, so the author can't cater and transfer details by the most adequate logical way. Please get past them and savor the book as a "spiritual dim sum."

CHAPTER 1: (GRATITUDE)
Question 1: How Do You Give Unconditionally?

The best gifts in life are those that are given without expectation in return. In such a society that is conquered by careerists, intending, fraud, those "precious gifts" ought to be multiplied much more times and be given to much more individual. Teaching children how to give unconditionally is the progress of building their moral basis of an anthropologist as well as cultivating a disinterested heart encased by an innocent soul. Besides, your kids are going to get started to believe in good values and gradually create good values for society. Altogether, let us have a look at a considerable role and a host of ways a kid lives an "unconditional giving" life.

The most important gift someone can give you is time. We live in a world of 'being Busy', where everyone will make excuses about why they cannot see you. The people who want to see you will make the time. You can't make everyone happy. Giving doesn't have to be financial. There are so many opportunities to be a positive impact on the world. The best gifts are the ones that we give freely. The trick is to get away from our own egos and accept that we may not get something back. Here are 25 tips on how to let go on the need for your gift to be returned, even with a simple "Thank You":

1. Give with a full heart:

All we really need is love and that begins with loving ourselves. If we are continually looking outside ourselves for gratification and acknowledgement we are not really giving with a full heart. When we have a full heart, truly love ourselves and know our worth, we can give so much more to others. We can know that blessing the other person is coming from a full heart and not a lack of love. With a full heart, we need nothing back because we are already full. Giving from this place is a gift in itself since we don't go into it expecting some form of love to be returned.

2. Give because you believe in abundance:

Abundance is a very large quantity of something. When you believe in abundance, you can give away nearly everything and know that you will still have plenty. When you are an abundant thinker, you see that material things as just that material. They are tangible items and don't really hold power over us unless we let them. When we give away money, clothing, presents and other items, we can truly live in abundance by believing at a heart level that we need nothing. We live in a place of knowing that gifting to others and sharing our material things can bless them in amazing ways. Take for example going to a developing country with extra clothing, shoes, toiletries and other items. When you gift those things to the people there, they are so appreciative and their lives are better because we believed in abundance and chose to give those things away. We bless people in amazing ways when we believe that we have enough and can constantly give things away.

3. Give simply knowing you want the other person's life to be better:

I think deep down we all want others to prosper and have wonderful lives. When we give simply because we want others to be happy we are filled with love and need nothing more in return. If you have something to give — whether its love, an item you own, or your time, you obviously feel that you have enough of that to give away. The reason to give in this situation is to make someone else's life better. If you have plenty, give some of that away and bless another person's life. Not only do you get the joy of giving, but you know that you are helping someone else feel full in some way. This creates a world around you where everyone is included and loved.

4. Give to people who don't deserve it:

In life, we run into people that rub us the wrong way. We start to resent them and may even resist having a relationship with them. We don't really care to interact with these people, let alone give them a gift. I think that this is the perfect time to give someone a gift. When we are in resistance and resentment we often look to get some type of revenge. This doesn't mean we plot their demise, but we may just ignore them or keep a part of ourselves inaccessible to them. That is also a form of revenge. The best way to get out of this cycle is to give a gift. When you give a gift, you automatically tell your mind and heart that you are full and don't hold any ill will or bad feelings towards that person. It's just like forgiveness. People don't always deserve it, but we forgive because it gives us freedom and ultimately helps us let go of anger and bitterness.

5. *Know that your gift will be returned in some way:*

When we give and hope to receive back from the same person, it can be seen as very narrow minded. The way the world works is that once you give something away, you automatically create space to be able to receive. Also, it is said that we receive back 10x what we give. It doesn't mean that we will receive back from the same person or organization to which we give. An example would be giving to a charity is that we don't get back from the charity necessarily (possibly a tax receipt), but we give because it feels good. That is one of the first ways we get back when we give. It gives us joy. That in itself is a gift. Often, we see the cycle go even further when we give here and receive from there. When you keep the cycle going it never stops, and you will always see your giving returned in some way. It may just be in a completely different manner that you expect. The other things you can do or teach your child to know how to give unconditionally consist of:

6. *Give money you can spare to someone who needs it and then pretend you never had it*

7. *Let someone tell a story without feeling the need to one-up them or tell your own.*

8. *Let someone vent, even if you can't offer a solution, just to be an ear without considering how well they listened to you last week.*

9. *Help someone who is struggling with difficult feelings by admitting you've felt the same thing without considering whether they'd be as open with you.*

10. *Ask, "What can I do to help you today?" Then let it go after following through.*

11. *Tell someone how you feel about them, even if it makes you feel vulnerable, just to let them know they're loved and not alone.*

12. *Apologize when you've acted selfishly, even if you don't like feeling wrong, because it will remind the other person they deserve to be treated with respect.*

13. *Let someone else educate you, even if you're tempted to stay closed minded, because you value their*

knowledge and appreciate their willingness to share it.

14. *Forgive someone who wronged you because you have compassion for them, not because you know they'll owe you.*

15. *Hold someone's hand when they feel vulnerable to let them know you haven't judged them.*

16. *Give your full attention to the person in front of you when you're tempted to let your thoughts wander just to show them their words are valuable.*

17. *Assume the best when you're tempted to suspect someone for no valid reason—even if they haven't always given you the benefit of the doubt.*

18. *Accompany someone to an appointment or drive them to an interview when they need support just to help them feel strong.*

19. Change your plans for someone you love if yours weren't too important without questioning whether they'd do the same for you.

20. Teach someone how to do something without taking a superior position because they've likely taught you many things, whether they were obvious or not.

21. Leave a thoughtful comment on someone's blog, not to build your readership but rather to show them how they affected you.

22. Tell someone you believe in their potential, even if they haven't always shown you the same support.
23. Say no when it would make you feel good to say yes, because sometimes being kind means pushing someone to step up and try harder.

24. Tell someone you know they meant well instead of using their mistake as an opportunity to manipulate their guilt.

25. I've left this one open for you to write. How do you give just to show you care?

*"Be grateful for the gifts you get back, they will come.
But also be grateful for the positive impact you have on
someone's life."*

CHAPTER 2: (CONFIDENCE)

Question 2: How would you knock obstacles down and get out of your comfort zone?

Seeing kids walk through the doorstep of life fully equipped with confidence, skill, and spirit to face every difficulties or challenge is what all parents hope to witness. However, that triumph cannot only be achieved overnight. It requires an operation of observing, listening, experiencing in real life, perceiving information and also storing, consolidating knowledge throughout their childhood. All those banal advice, as well as teachings which we continually pour into our kid's ears, every day are still nothing. The must is to balance between "Learn" and "Practice". We have to let them have more chances to embark on trials, not only those which are arisen from outdoor circumstances but also those created by ourselves, parents and adults in general so that they could be brave enough to encounter their own fear, accept and overcome it. To help you in drafting a specific orientation in educating your kids, pardon me to extract below here some manners which train your child skill, spirit as well as the confidence to be willing to admit obstacles and crash all of them on their current raw human racing line, even in future. They include:

1. *Love your child:*

This seems obvious, but it's probably the most important thing you can give your child. Even if you do it imperfectly, and who doesn't? Always dole out plenty of love. Your child needs to feel accepted and loved, beginning with the family and extending to other groups such as friends, schoolmates, sports teams, and community. If you yell or ignore or make some other parenting mistake, give your child a hug and tell her you're sorry and you love her. Unconditional love builds a strong foundation for confidence.

1. *Give praise where praise is due:*

It's important to give your child praise and positive feedback because children, especially young ones. Measure their worth and achievements by what you think. But be realistic in your praise. If a child fails at something or shows no talent at a particular skill, praise the effort, but don't unrealistically praise the results. Reassure your child that it's OK not to be able to do everything perfectly. Tell him that some things take repeated effort and practice. Sometimes it's ok to move on after you've given your best effort.

2. Help your child set realistic goals:

When your child is starting out in soccer, it is fine for her to think she'll eventually be on the Olympic team. But if she fails to make the varsity team in high school and still thinks she's an Olympic-caliber player, then she needs to focus on more realistic goals. Guide your child to set reasonable goals to help avoid feelings of failure. If the goal is a stretch, discuss some reachable short-term steps along the path.

3. Model self-love and positive self-talk:

You must love yourself before you can teach your child to love him or herself. You can model this behavior by rewarding and praising yourself when you do well. Whether you run a marathon, get a promotion at work or throw a successful dinner party, celebrate your successes with your children. Talk about the skills and talents and efforts needed for you to achieve those accomplishments. In the same conversation, you can remind your child of the skills he or she possesses and how they can be developed and used.

4. Teach resilience:

No one succeeds at everything all the time. There will be setbacks and failures, criticism and pain. Use these hurdles as learning experiences rather than dwelling on the events as failures or disappointments. The old adage, "Try, try, try again," has merit, especially in teaching kids not to give up. But, it's also important to validate your child's feelings rather than saying, "Oh, just cheer up," or, "You shouldn't feel so bad." This helps children learn to trust their feelings and feel comfortable sharing them. Children will learn that setbacks are a normal part of life and can be managed. If your child does poorly on a test, don't smother him with pity or tell him that he'll never be a good reader. Instead, talk about what steps he can take to do better next time. When he does succeed, he will take pride in his accomplishment.

5. Instill independence and adventure:

Self-confident children are willing to try new things without fear of failure. With younger children, you will need to supervise from the sidelines. Set up situations where she can do things for herself and make sure the situation is safe—but then give her space. For example, demonstrate how to make a sandwich and then let her try it on her own, without your hovering or intervening. Encourage exploration, whether it's a trip to a new park or new foods at mealtime. Day trips and outings, new hobbies, vacations and trips with teammates or schoolmates can all expand your child's horizons and build confidence in her ability to handle new situations.

6. Encourage sports or other physical activities:

No longer the sole domain of boys, sports help girls and boys build confidence. They learn that they can practice, improve and achieve goals. Other benefits: they learn to recognize their strengths, accept or strengthen their weaknesses, handle defeat, expand their circle of friends and learn teamwork. Another confidence-boosting bonus: they stay fit and learn to respect their bodies. Try to find a physical activity that he or she enjoys, whether it's dance, martial arts, biking or hiking.

7. Support their pursuit of a passion:

Everyone excels at something, and it is great when your child discovers that something. As a parent, respect and encourage your child's interests, even if they don't interest you. Praise your child when they accomplish something in their budding pursuits. If your son's talent is playing guitar in a band, support his interest, as long as it doesn't interfere with responsibilities like schoolwork. This doesn't mean you give free reign for your teenager to stay out all night or smoke pot in your garage, which brings us to the next tip.

8. Set rules and be consistent:

Children are more confident when they know who is in charge and what to expect. Even if your child thinks your rules are too strict, she will have confidence in what she can and can't do when you set rules and enforce them consistently. Every household will have different rules, and they will change over time based on your child's age. Whatever your household rules, be clear on what is important in your family. Learning and following rules gives children a sense of security and confidence. As children get older they may have more input on rules and responsibilities. But, it's important to remember that you are the parent, not a best friend. Someday when your child is feeling peer pressure, he or she may appreciate having the foundation and confidence to say, "No, I can't do that."

9. Coach relationship skills:

Confidence in relationships is key to your child's self-confidence. The most important initial relationship is the loving parent-child relationship. But as your child's social circle expands, you will help her see how her actions affect others, and help her learn to maintain an inner core of confidence when someone else's actions affect her. As a parent, it's not your role to "fix" every situation, but rather to teach your child the compassion, kindness, self-assertiveness and, yes, confidence to handle the ups and downs of relationships.

10. Appreciate effort no matter if they win or lose:

When you're growing up, the journey is more important than the destination. So whether your child makes the winning goal for his team or accidentally kicks it out of bounds, applaud their effort, Pickhardt says. They should never feel embarrassed for trying. "Over the long haul, consistently trying hard builds more confidence than intermittently doing well," he explains.

11. Let them figure out problems by themselves:

If you do the hard work for your child then they'll never develop the abilities or the confidence to figure out problems on their own. "Parental help can prevent confidence derived from self-help and figuring out on the child's own," Pickhardt explains. In other words, better that your child gets a few B's and C's rather than straight A's, so long as they are actually learning how to solve the problems and do the work.

12. Let them act their age:

Don't expect your child to act like an adult. "When a child feels that only performing as well as parents is good enough, that unrealistic standard may discourage effort," he says. "Striving to meet advanced age expectations can reduce confidence."

13. Encourage curiosity:

Sometimes a child's endless stream of questions can be tiresome, but it should be encouraged. Paul Harris of Harvard University told The

Guardian that asking questions is a helpful exercise for a child's development because it means they realize that "there are things they don't know ... that there are invisible worlds of knowledge they have never visited." When children start school, those from households that encouraged curious questions have an edge over the rest of their classmates because they've had practice taking in information from their parents, The Guardian reported, and that translates to taking in information from their teacher. In other words, they know how to learn better and faster.

14. Never criticize their performance:

Nothing will discourage your child more than criticizing his or her efforts. Giving useful feedback and making suggestions is fine — but never tell them they're doing a bad job. If your kid is scared to fail because they worry you'll be angry or disappointed, they'll never try new things. "More often than not, parental criticism reduces the child's self-valuing and motivation," says Pickhardt.

15. Open the door to new experiences:

Pickhardt says you, as a parent, have a responsibility to "increase life exposures and experiences so the child can develop confidence in coping with a larger world." Exposing children to new things teaches them that no matter how scary and different something seems, they can conquer it.

16. Don't tell them when you're worried about them:

Parental worry can often be interpreted by the child as a vote of no confidence, he says. "Expressing parental confidence engenders the child's confidence."

17. Praise them when they deal with adversity:

Life is not fair. It's hard, and every child will have to learn that at some point. When they do encounter hardships, Pickhardt says parents should point out how enduring these challenges will increase their resilience. It's important to remind your child that every road to success is filled with setbacks, he adds.

18. Offer your help and support, but not too much:

Giving too much assistance too soon can reduce the child's ability for self-help, says Pickhardt."Making parental help contingent on the child's self-help first can build confidence."

19. Applaud their courage to try something new:

Whether it's trying out for the travel basketball team or going on their first roller coaster, Pickhardt says parents should praise their kids for trying new things. He suggests saying something as simple as, "You are brave to try this!". Comfort comes from sticking to the familiar; courage is required to dare the new and different," he says.

20. Celebrate the excitement of learning:

When you're growing up, the journey is more important than the destination. So whether your child makes the winning goal for his team or accidentally kicks it out of bounds, applaud their effort, Pickhardt says. They should never feel embarrassed for trying. "Over the long haul, consistently trying hard builds more confidence than intermittently doing well," he explains.

21. Be authoritative, but not too forceful or strict:

When parents are too strict or demanding, the child's confidence to self-direct can be reduced. "Dependence on being told can keep the child from acting bold," he says.

22. Focus on the Glass Half Full:

If your child tends to feel defeated by disappointments, help her be more optimistic. Instead of offering glib reassurances to "look on the bright side," encourage her to think about specific ways to improve a situation and bring her closer to her goals, says Karen Reivich, PhD, coauthor of The Optimistic Child. If she's behind her classmates in reading, explain that everyone learns at her own pace, and offer to spend extra time reading with her. If she's crushed because she didn't get the lead in the second-grade play, don't say, "Well, I think you're a star." Instead, say, "I can see how disappointed you are. Let's come up with a plan for how you can increase the chances of getting the part you want next time."

23. Look for Ways to Help Others:

When children feel like they're making a difference -- whether it's passing out cups at preschool or taking cookies to a nursing home -- they feel more confident, says Dr. Brooks. It's good for kids to have their own household responsibilities, but it may be even more empowering for a young child to assist you with a project ("I could really use your help!"). He'll see firsthand that grown-up tasks require effort, and he'll be easier on himself when he has to work at things in the future, says Dr. Hirsh-Pasek.

24. Find Opportunities for Her to Spend More Time with Adults:

Kids like to hang out with their friends, but it's also important for them to be around a variety of grown-ups. Spending time with older people expands your child's world, forces her to talk to adults besides you, and gives her different ways of thinking. Research has also shown that having a close relationship with a particular grown-up. A teacher, an uncle, a babysitter, or a friend's parent makes children more resilient.

25. Fantasize About the Future:

If kids can envision themselves doing something important or fulfilling when they grow up, they're bound to feel more confident now. Talk to your child about how you, your spouse, and other adults he knows chose careers. Your child may dream of being a pop singer or an astronaut, but don't try to lower his expectations. Even if he changes his mind, the important thing is that he's thinking about his goals.

"Don't praise your child if he does something that he's supposed to do. When he brushes his teeth or throws his shirt into the hamper, for example, a simple "thank

CHAPTER 3: (PLEASURE)
Question 3: Why you need to appreciate the present moment?

An unconcerned but a global emerging problem and is also reminded or mentioned in a lot of "self-growing" books, such as "To Be or Not To Be", "Stop Worrying and Start Living". No doubt, it is "Worrying excessively" caused by pressure from jobs, routine life, friends' cheating, breaking in marriage and a billion of no-name reasons else, but on the whole, they will all lead you to the same dead-ends, including running short of vitality, being both psychologically exhausted and physically weary, even resulting in some diseases whose patients have never imagined that their real cause is overwhelmingly worrying. Those diseases may consist of gastritis, yellowed teeth, hypotension, heart failure and depression. Sounds so terrible, right? However, good news for you is that curing as well as preventing from this type of global syndrome by the habit of "Appreciating the present moment" are completely feasible. And the most amazing thing is that you can self- establish, form and maintain this habit inside of your own and your child, also. Right below, I will point out and break it down to you the reason wherefore does valuing present moment play a vital role in your life3 and how to forge this very useful habit.

When we stop to worry about our life, we're so blessed to even be alive that we fail to appreciate all of the things that are happening in our lives in the here and now. We look past the miracle and beauty of life and all the little things we have, and instead focus our mind's eye on the things we don't have. The food that we eat goes unappreciated until we can't afford to buy a meal. Similarly, the roof over our heads is unappreciated until we can't afford to have it and are effectively homeless. The clothes on our backs are similarly unappreciated. The point? We need to learn how to appreciate what we have right now because it can be gone in an instant. So how to get known the ways we can apply to appreciate our present moment more? While there might be hundreds of ways that we can do simple little things to appreciate our lives just a bit more, there are 10 very profound things that we can do today, right now, to harbor a bit more appreciation towards the things we have rather than the things we don't have.

1. Be grateful and count your blessings:

Gratitude is the pathway to happiness and success in life. The more we're grateful for the things we have, no matter how little they might be, the happier and sated we'll be in life. Why do we have to wait until something is taken from us to appreciate it in the here and now? Learn to be grateful and count your blessings, because tomorrow it might all be gone. Keep a journal and jot down your thoughts every single day. Write out everything that you're grateful for. Even if it's just for the air in your lungs and the heart beating continuously in your chest, write it down. If you can speak, read or write, then be grateful for that as well. Or, simply for the fact that you're six feet above ground.

2. Head to your local homeless shelter:

Find your local homeless shelter and go donate your time. Help to feed the people who can't afford to feed themselves. Look into their eyes and listen to their stories. They've lost it all for one reason or another. Some of them are alone in this world, and others have to care for small kids, and it's utterly heartbreaking to see this. If you really want to appreciate what you have, go see how the other half lives. Go witness what it's like to be in their shoes. Suddenly, your problems begin to dissipate once you see someone who can't even afford to house or feed themselves. It's one of the most moving experiences in life to do this and I highly recommend that you go contribute a little bit of your time to them.

3. Be present and live in the moment:

It's important to be present and to quite literally live in the moment if you're serious about appreciating what you have. There are so many miracles that are occurring all around us, that when we stop to actually pay attention, it a complete marvel and a wonder. The simple beauty of life and consciousness is so utterly astonishing that we have to be present and appreciate it. Take a walk in the park and literally listen to the birds chirping or smell the roses. It's hard to do when we're so immersed in our problems, but also a very important step to take to appreciate life. The truth is that life is a beautiful gift. It's here today, and can easily be gone tomorrow. Don't take that for granted.

4. Stop comparing yourself to others:

Sure, it's easy to compare ourselves to those who have more. It's quite simple to look to that car or house that we want and allow it to ruin our mood. We beat ourselves up over not having certain things. Why do we need to constantly compare ourselves to other people in this world? Why do we allow that to eliminate our chances for happiness? I'm not saying that I've never done it. But stop comparing yourself to others. There are far more people who have less than the people that have more. Appreciate what you have right now because those small things could also be gone tomorrow. Keep that in mind next time you longingly look at someone else and wildly diminish yourself compared to that person.

5. Downsize your life rather than upsizing it:

Sometimes, in order to appreciate what we have, we have to get back to the utter basics in life by downsizing. Get a smaller home. Buy a simpler car. Instead, use the money you save on experiences rather than the attainment of things. Life isn't about buying things, it's about experiencing all the wonder and joy out there in the world. It's easy to forget about all of that when you're constantly focused on paying for a costly lifestyle. Even if you can easily afford it right now, downsize anyhow. Put the money towards your savings or retirement. Help your kids or your family. Donate to a cause you love. Or travel the world to a foreign place and live amongst another culture.

6. Ask yourself different questions:

Sometimes, the questions that we ask ourselves preclude us from appreciating what we have. When you ask a poor question, you often get a poor answer. Instead, we need to ask better questions in an effort to get better answers. Instead of saying, when will I ever have something so nice? We should ask, what can I do today to help someone less fortunate than myself? We need to search for ways that we can improve our lives by first improving ourselves as human beings. Appreciation of things shouldn't arise from some monetary metric. Rather, it should come from the values that we harbor and the things that we can do in this world to make it a better place.

7. Visit terminally ill patients at the hospital:

Whether they are sick children or sick adults, there are people that are dying right now in hospitals close by. There are terminally ill children who haven't been given a chance in life. When you look into their eyes and realize that you've lived such a full life, you feel instantly guilty. However, this isn't meant to make you feel guilty for your life; it's meant to allow you to appreciate what you have. Even if you're not healthy, you're alive. Right now, you're alive. Visit those that are less fortunate and are fighting for the simple thing that so many of us take for granted: life.

8. Let go of hatred and negativity:

Hatred and negativity won't serve you whatsoever. You have to let go of it if you're serious about any semblance of appreciation or happiness in life. Hatred and anger are negative emotions that heavily weigh on the mind, constantly causing us to replay events over and over again, driving us crazy internally. There's almost no way to appreciate the things we have in life when we're so consumed by the ensuing negative energy created by things like hatred and animosity. There's no room for it in your life. Let it go. You don't need to forget. Just forgive. I know it's hard, but it's an important step in the healing and maturing process.

9. Smile even when you don't feel like it:

Studies prove that by simply smiling a genuine smile, also known as a Duchenne smile, we can lift ourselves out of depression and sadness, making us happier in life. It sounds like such a simple thing to do, but it's truly integral to any life that harbors appreciation for the simple little things. Look in the mirror and smile for 20 minutes per day. Smile a genuine smile by placing a pencil between your lips and holding it there. Think about all the good things you have and all of the wonderful people in your life. Think about all the things you've been given that so many others would only dream to have.

10. Focus on your faith and belief:

If you're a firm believer in God, Allah, Buddha or even the simplistic power and energy that binds us all, focus on your faith and your belief in that. If you can focus on your belief, you'll understand that God doesn't put things into your life that you can't handle. All of it is meant to serve you, to allow you to grow and mature, and to eventually reach new understandings about life. The importance of faith is second to none. Believe and it shall be given to you. Seek and ye shall find. Appreciate everything in your life, even the problems, because they were put there for a reason. You can't have sunshine and rainbows all the time. But when you have faith and belief, eventually, good things will go to pass as long as you don't give up hope.

11. Breathe deeply:

Inhale deeply, and exhale completely ten times. Deep breathing slows your thoughts, relaxes your nervous system, and brings you closer to your own intuition.

12. Use a mantra to change your mind-set:

Sha is a Sanskrit root word meaning peace, as in "shanti." Say "sham" slowly ten to twenty times. By combining sound, breath, and rhythm, mantra channels the flow of energy through the mind-body circuit and calms your nervous system and mind.

13. Zone out:

Spend a few minutes daydreaming. Your logical mind, the prefrontal cortex, is constantly planning, analyzing, and thinking about the future. Give it a rest, and just be for a little while; you'll feel refreshed.

14. Express your love:

Write a note or tell a loved one how you appreciate them. Communicating positive emotions lowers stress hormones, bad cholesterol, and blood pressure, and it strengthens immunity.

15. Rejuvenate your mind:

Close your eyes for a few moments. What do you see in the darkness of your mind's eye? Notice the patterns that form. This is a simple meditation that rejuvenates and refocuses your tired mind.

16. Explore healing aromas:

Plants like rosemary, lavender, and sage can improve our moods. Create your own natural spa. Put your favorite essential oils in a spray bottle with a little water.

17. Swap a thought:

Make a list of your positive traits and attributes. When you criticize yourself, refer to this list. Keep this pattern up and you'll transform your inner dialogue.

18. Allow yourself to be:

Accept all your feelings about your present situation. They are valid, whether you like them or not. Accepting your current situation is the first step to feeling happier.

19. Loving-kindness meditation:

Loving-kindness builds positive emotions, which increases mindfulness and purpose in life. Spend a few minutes letting feelings of love and kindness for someone wash over you.

20. Meditate:

When thoughts come, return to your breath without judging. Deep breathing clears your mind and decreases your stress levels, which will allow you to feel happier.

21. Declutter one spot:

Declutter one surface or area. Starting small is easier. But when your home and workspace are clear from clutter, your mind feels more spacious.

22. Lighten up:

Once a day, laugh at yourself. When you make a mistake, see the humor in your error. Laughing is great medicine, it improves your mood, and it relieves stress and tension.

23. Stretch your body:

Sitting in a chair? Push away from your desk. Inhale, and as you exhale, bend forward, moving your ribs toward your thighs. Breathe deeply. Get out of your mind and into your body and the present moment.

24. Stretch your breath:

Hold onto the back of your chair, and breathe deeply. This opens up your rib cage and lungs, allowing you to breathe more deeply. The added oxygen to your brain will make you feel alive and alert.

25. Give yourself a massage:

Use coconut oil or sesame oil on your skin, massage it on your whole body, and then take a warm shower to help your skin absorb the oil. This is a home spa treatment that is used all over India. Touch is calming, and you can reap its benefits without buying expensive massages.

26. Take a bath:

Relax and enjoy the simple pleasure of a warm bath. Light some candles, and put on your favorite music. Soothe your body with this simple ritual. Why dream about getting away when you can create a calming environment in your home?

27. Place your palms over your eyelids:

This relaxes your eyes and mind. This is especially helpful if you have a headache or feel fatigued.

28. Practice Yoga Nidra (Yogic Sleep):

Take ten minutes to relax your whole body completely and then each part of your body in turn. This magical practice is as efficient as taking a longer nap.

29. Eat with complete attention:

Put away all your screens. Savor your meal by noticing all its tastes and textures. You'll improve your digestion and feel more relaxed as a result.

30. Move every day:

Even if you have very little time. You only need five minutes to stretch or walk outside. Building a little movement into your day is better for your health than one longer weekly workout.

"Your happiness isn't dependent on where you live, how much you weigh, or what you do for work. The key to happiness is appreciating what you have at this moment."

CHAPTER 4: (PEACE)

*Question 4: How to foster
your positive soul?*

A life which is glittered by roses, fulfilled with happiness and easy-going is what all people desire to walk on and try hard to find out through working day and night, pulling an all-nighter, getting up at a crack of dawn, having nerves breaking times because of pondering about livelihood. But Lord! They are all wrong. Happiness is not emanated from those posh vanity valuables but from tranquility in the soul, a light-hearted mind and "accepting" behavior. On top of that, we need a positiveness in our spirit, our attitudes, and our gestures, also. The well-known entrepreneur, Ph.D. Alan Phan have asserted a very deep perspective about the original value of the matter, "Money is nothing to me, but all that I adore needing money." A doctor has proclaimed that that vanity bling-bling cannot value humankind's happiness but he has never protected the allegation considers being thoughtless to all earthly businesses. This is because all material in the universe is "bonded" to each other by one or more indispensable inevitable relations by each level of relationships. You can easily recognize here a connection between fostering a positive spirit and appreciating the present moment (As I did mention in Chapter Three). Valuating minutely is a priority minimum thing that you ought to do if you want to possess optimistic morale as well as positive thinking to be always staying calm in front of any issue. No matter how hard it could be. Thus, how could we do to build up optimistic habits and become optimists which are a derivation of those who would obtain a happy life in the soul? A list of very useful remedies below would help you in unwinding that query.

1. Start the day with positive affirmation:

How you start the morning sets the tone for the rest of the day. Have you ever woken up late, panicked, and then felt like nothing good happened the rest of the day? This is likely because you started out the day with a negative emotion and a pessimistic view that carried into every other event you experienced. Instead of letting this dominate you, start your day with positive affirmations. Talk to yourself in the mirror, even if you feel silly, with statements like,

"Today will be a good day" or "I'm going to be awesome today." You'll be amazed how much your day improves.

2. Focus on the good things, however small:

Almost invariably, you're going to encounter obstacles throughout the day. There's no such thing as a perfect day. When you encounter such a challenge, focus on the benefits, no matter how slight or unimportant they seem. For example, if you get stuck in traffic, think about how you now have time to listen to the rest of your favorite podcast. If the store is out of the food you want to prepare, think about the thrill of trying something new.

3. Find humor in bad situations:

Allow yourself to experience humor in even the darkest or most trying situations. Remind yourself that this situation will probably make for a good story later and try to crack a joke about it. Say you're laid off; imagine the most absurd way you could spend your last day, or the most ridiculous job you could pursue next, like kangaroo handler or bubblegum sculptor.

4. Turn failures into lessons:

You aren't perfect. You're going to make mistakes and experience failure in multiple contexts, at multiple jobs and with multiple people. Instead of focusing on how you failed, think about what you're going to do next time, turn your failure into a lesson. Conceptualize this in concrete rules. For example, you could come up with three new rules for managing projects as a result.

5. Transform negative self-talk into positive self-talk:

Negative self-talk can creep up easily and is often hard to notice. You might think I'm so bad at this or I shouldn't have tried that. But these thoughts turn into internalized feelings and might cement your conceptions of yourself. When you catch yourself doing this, stop and replace those negative messages with positive ones. For example, I'm so bad at this becomes Once I get more practice, I'll be way better at this. I shouldn't have tried becomes. That didn't work out as planned, maybe next time.

6. Focus on the present:

I'm talking about the present, not today, not this hour, only this exact moment. You might be getting chewed out by your boss, but what in this exact moment is happening that's so bad? Forget the comment he made five minutes ago. Forget what he might say five minutes from now. Focus on this one, individual moment. In most situations, you'll find it's not as bad as you imagine it to be. Most sources of negativity stem from a memory of a recent event or the exaggerated imagination of a potential future event. Stay in the present moment.

7. Find positive friends, mentors and co-workers:

When you surround yourself with positive people, you'll hear positive outlooks, positive stories and positive affirmations. Their positive words will sink in and affect your own line of thinking, which then affects your words and similarly contributes to the group. Finding positive people to fill up your life can be difficult, but you need to eliminate the negativity in your life before it consumes you. Do what you can to improve the positivity of others, and let their positivity affect you the same way.

8. Focus on the good things:

Challenging situations and obstacles are a part of life. When you're faced with one, focus on the good things no matter how small or seemingly insignificant they seem. If you look for it, you can always find the proverbial silver lining in every cloud, even if it's not immediately obvious. For example, if someone cancels plans, focus on how it frees up time for you to catch up on a TV show or other activity you enjoy.

9. Practice gratitude:

Practicing gratitude has been shown to reduce stress, improve self-esteem, and foster resilience even in very difficult times. Think of people, moments, or things that bring you some kind of comfort or happiness and try to express your gratitude at least once a day. This can be thanking a co-worker for helping with a project, a loved one for washing the dishes, or your dog for the unconditional love they give you.

10. Keep a gratitude journal:

Studies Trusted Source have found that writing down the things you're grateful for can improve your optimism and sense of well-being. You can do this by writing in a gratitude journal every day, or jotting down a list of things you're grateful for on days you're having a hard time.

11. Open yourself up to humor:

Studies have found that laughter lowers stress, anxiety, and depression. It also improves coping skills, mood, and self-esteem. Be open to humor in all situations, especially the difficult ones, and give yourself permission to laugh. It instantly lightens the mood and makes things seem a little less difficult. Even if you're not feeling it;

pretending or forcing yourself to laugh can improve your mood and lower stress.

12. Spend time with positive people:

Negativity and positivity have been shown to be contagious. Consider the people with whom you're spending time. Have you noticed how someone in a bad mood can bring down almost everyone in a room? A positive person has the opposite effect on others. Being around positive people has been shown to improve self-esteem and increase your chances of reaching goals. Surround yourself with people who will lift you up and help you see the bright side.

13. Identify your areas of negativity:

Take a good look at the different areas of your life and identify the ones in which you tend to be the most negative. Not sure? Ask a trusted friend or colleague. Chances are, they'll be able to offer some insight. A co-worker might notice that you tend to be negative at work. Your spouse may notice that you get especially negative while driving. Tackle one area at a time.

14. Start every day on a positive note:

Create a ritual in which you start off each day with something uplifting and positive. Here are a few ideas:

- Tell yourself that it's going to be a great day or any other positive affirmation.
- Listen to a happy and positive song or playlist.
- Share some positivity by giving a compliment or doing something nice for someone.

15. Start by looking at how you carry yourself:

Do you slouch a lot? Do you frown a lot? Are you always distracted? All these things affect how others see you, along with how you see yourself. Let's face it- what would YOU think if you saw someone slouching over and yawning in his/her seat? To be positive, you should look positive.

16. Think good thoughts:

Don`t judge others or yourself...this only creates negativity, and who wants to be around a negative person? Maybe to get on your good side so they won`t get dissed by you- but really? No one wants a negative friend. Try to come up with a catchy thought that you can think every day at least ONCE. Something that`ll make you smile, laugh, or just feel warm inside. Ex: "Today is a beautiful and inspirational day" or..."I am love, and love is me" Something like that is not only positive, but true as well. This is very good for your mental and emotional health.

17. Appreciate your friends and yourself:

Try this exercise- the next time you get into a fight with your friend, write a list of all the GREAT things about your friend instead of the negative. By reminding yourself of how great your friend really is- you`ll realize that the fight you two just had is not worth risking your friendship. Take the time to say thank you for the little things your friends do for you, and to compliment them sincerely- they`ll appreciate it, and it`ll make YOU feel good inside as well!

18. Show your family you care:

Being positive doesn't exclude your family! No matter how much you may hate them at times, you`ll always love them, so take the time to talk to them, laugh with them, buy them things and just say I love you. If you haven't done this in a while, and you don't want it to look sudden, slowly work your way in by just talking to them casually. To really influence things, leave little notes of appreciation or kindhearted humor on the table before you go to school (if you're a teenager) for your parents!

19. Watch what you eat:

To keep your energy flowing positively through your body, eating 3 solid meals and having lots of fruits and veggies really does help. If you're not sure how to get a lot of fruit/veggies in your meal, try some V8 (they have drinks and soups out that you'll positively love!) It gives you the energy and will power to get through work, school, or just a simple day!

20. Take time off for self-discovery:

To stay healthy mentally, take a day off from school/work to just hang low. During this time you can meditate, take a nice bubble bath, go to the zoo, or just take a walk to the store around the corner! A more simple things you do, a more positive you are.

21. Get a hobby:

Once you find your passion and learn about it, it's even easier to stay positive since you'll be happy doing it! Relax. Doing things like yoga, meditating, listening to nature, and going for walks really are great for your mind and spirit. Just imagine-being positive will flourish while doing something as relaxing as yoga in an enchanting park or spiritual garden! It's almost impossible to be negative while doing any of these things because you're giving your mind time to relax and slow down, letting the simple joys of the day unfold.

22. Make up a song that'll get you through the day:

This works in more ways than one, and even if you don't believe you can sing or write, it's still fun to try! Get a blank piece of paper, a pen/pencil and start to write a song about nature, love, religion, or even your prospective on life(a positive one at that)! Make sure everything in the song is positive and upbeat so whenever you're feeling down you can sing it to remind yourself how great life really is! If you truly believe you cannot sing just remember- anything is possible when you believe in yourself! (and it's true!)If you feel daring, write a copy of this song and frame it, putting it in your room like it's a poem! This way, you'll always be able to see it- no matter what!

23. Study intuition books:

These books are highly recommended for someone who wants to start a positive life style because it'll teach you all about the magical wonders of the human body, mind, and spirit, which will automatically impress and dazzle you to becoming even more positive! One highly recommended book is: "101 ways to Jump-Start Your Intuition" by John Holland. Your intuition is key to a happy life- and by studying it and living by its standards, you'll begin to realize how amazing life REALLY is! (plus we all have intuition as well, it's like a gut feeling- but once you start to learn about it, it goes so much deeper than that.)

24. Surround yourself with positive people:

Join a laughter or meditation class or a nearby yoga club, interact with people who like you are looking for positiveness and attaining it. This will not only improve your inner happiness but make it more enjoyable.

25. Ask yourself, "Do I think positively?"

Not sure whether you're a negative nelly? Take this well-being quiz, which not only gives you a score on "positivity," but can help you identify the other skills that can most help you improve your happiness and well-being. If you're someone who needs to work on your positivity, keep reading.

26. Strengthen your memory for positive information:

Did you know that you may be able to increase your positivity just by memorizing lists of positive words? It's because when you force your brain to use positive words frequently, you make these words (and their basic meaning) more accessible, more connected, and more easily activated in your brain. So when you go to retrieve a word or idea from your memory, positive ones can come to the top more easily.

27. Strengthen your brain's ability to work with positive information:

Once your brain has built strong neural networks for positive words, try to extend these networks by asking your brain to use positive information in new ways. For example, you could memorize positive words and set an alarm that reminds you to recall these words, in reverse order, an hour later. Or, you could print out these words on cards, cut them into two pieces, shuffle them all together and then find each card's match. For example, the word "laughter" would be cut into "laug" and "hter." To match the word pieces, your brain has to search through lots of positive information to find what it's looking for. This positive memory recall task may make it easier when you try to think positive.

28. Condition yourself to experience random moments of positivity:

Did you know that you can condition yourself for positivity? If you've ever taken an intro to psychology course, you've probably heard about the study of Pavlov's dog. Here is a quick refresher: Pavlov had a dog. Pavlov would ring a bell to tell his dog that it was almost feeding time. Like most dogs, Pavlov's dog would get really excited when he was about to get fed. So he'd drool all over the place. What happened? Well, suddenly Pavlov's dog started getting excited just by the sound of that bell, even when food wasn't present. Eating food and the sound of the bell became linked in the dog's brain. Something as meaningless as a bell was now making the dog excited. This effect is called classical conditioning. It's the idea that when two stimuli are repeatedly paired, the response that was first elicited by the second stimulus (food) is now elicited by the first stimulus alone (the bell). This happens all the time without us even realizing it. For example, the favorite food for many of us is something that we ate as a child with our families. What likely happened was the positive feelings of being with family and the particular food got paired in our brains. As a result, we now get the warm-fuzzy feelings that we got from spending time with family just from eating the food alone, even if our family is not currently present when we eat it.

29. Think positive, but not too much, and think negative when you need to:

Of course, thinking positive has its benefits. But thinking positive isn't always the best response. Negative thoughts sometimes have benefits, too. When we are sad or grieving, thinking negative thoughts and showing the emotions that these thoughts create helps us communicate to others that we need their support and kindness. When we are treated unfairly and get angry, our thoughts can help motivate us to take action, make changes in our lives, and change the world. Casually pushing these negative emotions aside without seriously considering their origins can have negative consequences. So when you focus on the negative, ask yourself, is this negative emotion resulting in action that improves your life? If so, then keep it. If not, then work on changing it.

30. Savor the good moments:

Too often we let the good moments pass, without truly celebrating them. Maybe your friend gives you a small gift or a colleague makes you laugh. Do you stop to notice and appreciate these small pleasures that life has to offer? If not, then you could benefit from savoring. Savoring just means holding onto the good thoughts and emotions we have. You can savor by holding on to the emotions you're feeling in positive moments. Or you can savor by thinking about positive experiences from long ago. Savoring is a great way to develop a long-lasting stream of positive thoughts and emotions.

31. Generate positive emotions by watching fun videos:

The broaden-and-build theory suggests that experiencing positive emotions builds our psychological, intellectual, and social resources, allowing us to benefit more from our experiences. So how do we infuse our lives with small bursts of positive emotion? One way is to watch positive or fun videos. Watching cat videos or inspirational videos can generate a quick boost of positive emotions that can help fuel an upward spiral of positive emotions.

32. Stop minimizing your successes:

We have a bad habit of downplaying our successes and not fully appreciating our wins. For example, we may say, "Anyone could memorize positive words," or "I didn't increase my happiness as much I wanted to." But this fails to recognize the effort that you put in effort that not everyone would put in. These phrases minimize your small successes instead of celebrating them.

"Be careful not to start thinking you're a complete failure just because you're not a complete success in all the ways you hoped to be. You win some, you lose some. That's life."

CHAPTER 5: (WISDOM)

Question 5: What did you learn today?

K nowledge is essentially considered to be an endless spiritual subsistent stock that has been crystalized through each historical period since the primitive age. Still, there are a majority of pretentious individuals which assume that they are "anthropologists" and are "prominent" in all aspects of life whilst they don't realize that each of them is just a "drop" in the vast of Pacific, a "tiny sand" on the extreme dry surface of Sahara, or even just a molecule of the infinite galaxy. The reason that kind of mindset gradually transforms into tangible gestures is their habit of unthoughtfully mimicking others. They approach information very fast and on time but they don't tend to perceive information from many waves of news. As a result, that habit causes heating controversies, debates or even all-out "battles", just to protect their conservative opinion which they have not ever been a witness to demonstrate their point. It will be probably more dangerous when that old-schooled way of thinking and criticizing has formed inside of your mind since you were a child. So, as a mom or a dad who truly hopes their children become "prominent figures" and make incredible things for the society as well as themselves, I empathize with your persistent anxiety while trying to "unearth" a way to train them to be such wise persons like that. There will be a recommended list of mine to you that comprises of what you should and should not do to help your kids in establishing a route of cultivating and developing correctly wonderful wisdom.

What you should do:

1. Do teach social skills:

A 20-year study by researchers at Pennsylvania State and Duke University shows a positive correlation between children's social skills in kindergarten and their success in early adulthood. Teaching your kids how to resolve issues with friends, share their belongings, listen without interrupting, and help others in the home is a great place to start.

2. Don't overprotect:

In today's age of helicopter parenting, many parents (including myself) have difficulty allowing our kids to solve problems, but rather rush to fix challenges for them. Drawing on a Harvard University study, Julie Lythcott-Haims argues that allowing kids to make mistakes and develop resilience and resourcefulness is critical in setting them up for success.

3. Do get your kids involved in academics early (then encourage independence when they are older:

Research shows that reading to your children and teaching them math early can greatly impact achievement in later years. However, it is best to start weaning kids off homework help later in elementary school, as helping your child with homework can actually stunt their development. Parents should always communicate interest in their children's schooling, but encourage them to take charge of their work independently.

4. Don't let them languish in front of a screen:

Too much screen time has been linked to childhood obesity, irregular sleep patterns, and behavioral issues. In addition, a 2017 study by Greg L. West at the University of Montreal revealed that playing "shooter" games can damage the brain, causing it to lose cells. So what can we do about the ever-so-helpful digital babysitter that so many of us rely on? According to the American Academy of Pediatrics, entertainment "screen time" should be limited to two hours a day.

5. Do set high expectations:

Harnessing data from a national survey, a UCLA team discovered that the expectations parents hold for their kids have a huge effect on achievement. The study found that, by the time they were four, almost all the children in the highest performing study group had parents who expected them to attain a college degree.

6. Don't spend too much time praising innate qualities such as intelligence or looks:

"Wow, you got an A without even studying? You are so smart! "A Stanford University study shows that praising children with statements like the above and focusing on their intelligence, can actually lead to underperformance. As an alternative parenting strategy, parents are encouraged to offer praise that focuses on the effort kids expend to overcome problems and challenges by demonstrating grit, persistence, and determination.

7. Do assign chores:

There is a significant body of evidence that shows that chores are beneficial for childhood development. Yet, in a Braun Research poll, just 28 percent of parents said they regularly assign chores to their kids. A University of Minnesota analysis of data found that the best predictor of success in young adulthood was whether children had performed chores as young as three or four.

8. Don't tune out:

According to a survey by Common Sense Media, 28 percent of teens said their parents were addicted to their mobile devices. Another recent study by AVG discovered that 32 percent of children surveyed felt unimportant when their parents were distracted by their phones. As the first generation of parents with 24/7 access to the Internet, it is important for us to know when to disconnect and focus on the family.

9. Do strive for a peaceful, loving home:

Children in high-conflict families tend to fare worse than children of parents that get along, according to a University of Illinois study review. Creating a loving, supportive environment is a staple of healthy, productive offspring. If you do have an argument with a spouse, it is recommended to model fair fighting, boundary-setting, and a focus on reconciliation and resolution.

10. Don't be too hard (or too soft):

Diana Baumrind, in her groundbreaking 1966 study, distinguished between authoritarian (very strict), permissive (very lenient), and authoritative (equally disciplined and loving) parents. In short, authoritarian parents are too hard, permissive parents are too soft, and authoritative are just right. When a child models their authoritative parents, they learn emotion regulation skills and social understanding that are critical for success.

11. Read books to your kid:

Start reading to him even if he does not understand the words. This gives him a head start in developing language skills. Kids who are read to when young are more likely to develop a lifelong interest in reading, do well in school, and succeed in adult life. Reading books is one of the most important activity that make kids smart.

12. Talk to your kid:

This develops your child's strong language skills. Also, listen to your child when he's talking. This reinforces his effort to communicate and develops his facility for language. A study shows that kids who experienced more conversation at home had greater brain activity and verbal attitude. Ask questions and wait for responses instead of engaging in a one-way narration. With babies, you can exchange coos and silly faces.

13. The best toys for your young child should not necessarily be expensive:

Choose toys that can be played more than one way – those that allow your child to have fun in various ways with the help of her imagination. See more tips on how to choose toys to make your child smart.

14. Make your child a reader:

The love for reading brings so many benefits for your child. It is one of the most important quality you can develop on your child for him to grow up smart. Reading develops your child's appetite for knowledge. The more your child learns from reading, the more he wants to know. By being a reader early in life, your child is well-prepared to grasp the complexities of mathematics, science, history, engineering, mechanics, political science, and other knowledge necessary for a productive life. See more benefits of reading.

15. Encourage your kid to exercise:

Physical exercise does not only make your kid strong, but it also makes your kid smart! Exercise increases the flow of blood to the brain and builds new brain cells. Exercise is good for adults' mental sharpness, but it has a more long-lasting effect on your kid's still developing brain. See more benefits of exercise on children's brain.

16. Make music a part of your child's life:

Studies have shown that listening to music can boost memory, attention, motivation and learning. It can also lower stress that is destructive to your kid's brain. A study has also shown that children's brains develop faster with music training.

17. Let your child see you doing smart things:

Kids learn by modeling adult's behavior. If he sees you engaged in reading books, writing, making music, or doing creative things, he will imitate you, and in the process make himself smart.

18. Allow your child to get bored:

According to Julia Robinson, Education and Training Director of the Independent Association of Prep Schools, it is okay for your child to get bored. Learning to be bored is part of preparing for adulthood. Your child should learn to enjoy "quiet reflection" instead of forcing him to fill his days with activities.

19. Make sure your child gets enough sleep:

A number of studies show a correlation in the amount of sleep and grades. If continued long enough, sleep issues can cause permanent problems.

20. Give your child a growth mindset:

According to psychiatrist Joe Brewster, kids should be encouraged to see learning as the process of becoming better at something, instead of having a fixed mind-set of his intelligence. When your child fails, he should see it as an opportunity for growth, instead of seeing himself as a failure.

What you should not do:

1. Stop coddling your child:

If you want him to be a leader, according to leadership expert Tim Elmore. Also, give him projects that require patience, so he learns to master certain disciplines. Find more tips in this Forbes article.

2. Stop micromanaging your child:

Don't constantly correct her. Let her discover things for herself to nurture her creative and innovative thinking.

3. Stop stressing out your child:

Kids who are stressed in their first 3 years tend to be sensitive to stress. Their brains are hard-wired to overreact to stressful situations and they end up hyperactive, anxious, impulsive and oftentimes neurotic. Also don't show your child that you are too stressed because it can be contagious. Click here for effects of stress on your kid's brain.

4. Stop wasting your time looking for a manual, because there isn't any:

There is absolutely nothing in this world that can really prepare you for parenthood. The bottom line of becoming a parent is you'll lose autonomy, sacrifice your leisure and face relationship challenges with your parenting partner. But in due course of time you will soon realize that these challenges were worth your time and effort because being a parent brings immense joy and enrichment in your life.

5. Stop pretending to be a perfect parent, because nobody in this world is:

While it's tempting to simply impart your wisdom to your children, it's important to resist this urge and engage them in a dialogue. Let them speak for themselves, in school or with others. Let them adopt perspectives and use their own reason instead of just fulfilling tasks or learning facts. As a parent you can afford to be demanding, yet responsive. There is no harm in setting high standards and expectations, but at the same time, it becomes imperative that you are emotionally available and responsive to children's needs too. You learn to get comfortable reasoning with your kids, giving them freedom to explore, and letting them fail and ultimately make their own choices.

6. Stop being a helicopter Parent:

To have kids is one of the most important decisions in our life. Therefore it's very natural for any parent to become highly sensitive to every needs of their ward. But in our eagerness to be the BEST that we can, we end up being a "helicopter parent". Julie Lythcott-Haims in her book ,"How to raise an adult" shares that: "Helicopter parents are so obsessed with making sure everything goes perfectly with their children that they often feel constantly exhausted and depressed, worried that they aren't doing enough for their kids. Often the parent's ego finds expression in their children. Everything the children do how they dress, how they perform, is seen as a reflection of the parents.

7. Stop expecting your kid to understand your thing:

Your kids need to understand that apart from being a parent you are a human too. A human that is fallible, lousy and not perfect. Kids do have a natural tendency to get very emotional with the problems of their parents. But that doesn't mean you start involving them. You need to handle your own shit because your teenager might have a pile of his own. Not only this, parent often makes the mistake of trying to live a vicarious life through their children. We all regret little things from our teenage years, and as a parent as soon as we sense an opportunity to prevent it from happening in our kid's life, we don't hesitate in pouncing on it — rarely the smart move.

8. Stop pushing your kids to always toe your line:

Jennifer Senior in her book "All joy and no fun" writes: "The modern world is an unsteady, unpredictable place. No one knows exactly what the future will bring. Jobs in the West that seem steady today may soon be outsourced, and others may be automated or mechanized." Therefore, in order to secure a good job, parents are desperately trying to encourage their offspring to master as many skills as possible. They want to cover all the bases.

9. Stop hitting them:

No denying that there exists vast cultural differences on this sensitive issue. Still it doesn't make much sense using hitting as an escape to wriggle yourself out of extremely sticky situations. What's the underlying message when you are hitting your kid? That you are comfortable using the violence as a medium if someone is not toeing your line. You are more vulnerable stretching the extreme corners of your tranquility zone if you find yourself capable of dominating the other dialogue partner.

10. Stop propagating the bribe based parenting:

If your kid is promised the bribe of an ice cream bucket for helping his little brother in exam preparation, you are probably missing the implicit moral hazard here. If left unattended this has potential to easily develop into a habit, where your kid is unable to appreciate the significance of personal responsibility and accountability. Instead he would be found more responsive to impending rewards.

11. Stop excessive use of mobile devices both by you and by them:

With the exponential explosion of digital technology, parenting has become far more challenging. And there is absolutely no escaping from strings of problems that emanates from its widespread use. As a parent you show your highest concern regarding the excessive use of digital devices by your kids. But conveniently forget that you were the one who encouraged to use it as a tool to keep them engaged, so that you could give more attention to your own preferred activities or devices.

12. Stop messing with their playtime:

Playtime, for them, is very important. Therefore, it should be unstructured, spontaneous and based on their decisions – not the parent's. Play is an opportunity for children to develop, as they try new things, test hypotheses and observe the world around them. They need a certain degree of freedom in order to do this constructively. Children learn to solve conflicts, find compromises and negotiate in play. From deciding on roles when playing hospital to working out how to build a tree house together, kids ensure their play session doesn't end in chaos and tears. "Play is the highest form of research." Albert Einstein said.

13. Stop treating your teenage kids like grown up:

Jennifer Senior in her book "All joy and no fun" makes it amply clear. Parents often think the ideal way to bring up a teenager is to treat them like an adult, permitting them to make their own choices and enjoy their own freedom. However, this is very risky, as adolescents are vastly different from full-grown adults. First, they don't react to rational arguments like most adults. No matter how logical a proposition, an adolescent is likely to respond emotionally. They are extremely hungry for experimentation. When given freedom, they stretch it as far as they can. Allow them to drink alcohol and they'll probably keep at it until they're fall-down drunk.

14. Stop telling your kids that they are special:

Kids shouldn't simply be told that they are special and can achieve anything. They need to learn to put in the hard work to achieve their dreams. This can be easily taught with simple responsibilities like daily chores. This will teach them autonomy, perseverance and accountability. As a consequence they will be better placed to appreciate the fruits of their own labor. Paul Harvey, a professor at University of New Hampshire finds that: "a great source of frustration for people with a strong sense of entitlement is unmet expectations. They often feel entitled to a level of respect and rewards that aren't in line with their actual ability and effort levels, and so they might not get the level of respect and rewards they are expecting." "They've been led to believe, perhaps through overzealous self-esteem building exercises in their youth that they are somehow special but often lack any real justification for this belief."

15. Stop measuring the worth of your kid by their intellectual capabilities:

Parents, especially those who are highly educated, are more likely to see their children's intellectual capabilities over their children's actual interests. If a child has the intelligence and innate skills needed to be a medical doctor but would rather work as an artist, then that kid will never be a happy (or even a good) physician. Helping children find their passion means teaching them to listen to their intuition. Parents have to step back, see their kids for who they truly are and allow them to follow what interests them, not just what they're good at. After all, kids will only put effort into something they enjoy. If you want them to be successful, you have to teach your children to find their own way. "Everybody is a genius. But if you judge a fish by its ability to climb a tree, it will live its whole life believing that it is stupid." Albert Einstein said.

"Knowing when to praise and when to criticize a kid show his or her parent's real care for his or her growth of mind."

CONCLUSION

Throughout five introspective questions in this book, I hope you would generally visualize a route of educating your kids more effectively, but don't forget that besides letting your child find their answers for those questions, you should also give them advice and let themselves suppose ways to tackle those troubles. The priorities of a parent are the endless care for their child as the burning desire to set aside the best things ever for those kids. Nevertheless, to become an advanced and generous father or mother in the modern age when kids and teenagers tend to be so psychologically impulsive and do crazy things, always be a mentor and a constructor of them and let them have all rights to make their own decisions in their own life. In conclusion, I would truly love to give great gratitude to all those readers who have been through this book with me. I hope that you would consider it to be a "handbook" that is in any help to you, your relatives, and most importantly your child.

ABOUT THE AUTHOR

Sheila Rosenberg was a teacher of English Literature and published in the area of Victorian Studies. She then moved into teaching, developing and publishing in English as a second language and in 2011 received an OBE for her contribution to ESOL teaching.

An anthropologist by training, Sheila received her B.A. from McGill University and her M.A. from the University of Paris. She joined Ryerson, and has taught numerous business and technical communication courses at the School of Professional Communication and the G. Raymond Chang School of Continuing Education. Before joining Ryerson, Sheila taught at Sheridan College, Seneca College, and Vanier College in Quebec.

www.ingramcontent.com/pod-product-compliance
Lightning Source LLC
La Vergne TN
LVHW040036180525
811579LV00009B/473